easy going
locker zu super Noten

Schulaufgaben

von bayerischen Gymnasien

Englisch 8

mit Lösungen

DURCHBLICKER Lernstudio Arndt

Schulaufgaben von bayerischen Gymnasien

Verfügbare Titel

☺ **Mathematik** für Klasse **5, 6, 7, 8, 9, 10, 11** und **12**

☺ **Physik** für Klasse **8, 9** und **10**

☺ **Chemie** für Klasse **8, 9** und **10**

☺ **Englisch** für Klasse **5, 6, 7, 8, 9, 10** und **11/12**

☺ **Französisch** für Klasse **6, 7, 8** und **9**

☺ **Deutsch** für Klasse **5, 6, 7** und **8**

☺ **Latein** für Lernjahr **1, 2** und **3**

Schulaufgaben bayerischer Realschulen

Verfügbare Titel

☺ **Mathematik** für Klasse **5, 6, 7II / III, 8II / III, 9II / III** und **10II / III**

☺ **Englisch** für Klasse **5, 6, 7, 8, 9** und **10**

☺ **Deutsch** für Klasse **5, 6, 7** und **8**

Schulproben von bayerischen Mittelschulen

Verfügbare Titel

☺ **Mathematik** für Klasse **5** und **6**

☺ **Englisch** für Klasse **5** und **6**

☺ **Deutsch** für Klasse **5** und **6**

Schulproben von bayerischen Grundschulen

Verfügbare Titel

☺ **Mathematik** für Klasse **3** und **4**

☺ **Deutsch** für Klasse **3** und **4**

☺ **Heimat- und Sachunterricht (HSU)** für Klasse **3** und **4**

Vorwort

Liebe Schüler, liebe Eltern,

seit der G8-Reform zur Verkürzung der Schulzeit ist Englisch praxisnäher und lebendiger geworden. Diese

Schulaufgaben von bayerischen Gymnasien

Englisch 8

zeigen, welche Aufgabentypen und welcher Schwierigkeitsgrad im G8-Gymnasium in Bayern verlangt werden. Ein großer Teil der Aufgaben habe ich als Englischlehrerin selber entworfen. Original-Schulaufgaben von Nachhilfeschülern unseres ***Durchblicker Lernstudio Arndt*** bilden die Grundlage der Aufgaben in diesem Buch. Wer diese Schulaufgaben konsequent durcharbeitet, dem sind bessere Noten sicher. Durch Übung kommt jeder Schüler zum Erfolg.

In der 8. Klasse werden drei Schulaufgaben geschrieben. Oft heißen diese dann „Großer Leistungstest“. Im vorliegenden Band finden sich pro Schulaufgabe jeweils zwei Prüfungen. Die sechs hier gestellten Schulaufgaben mit Lösungen entsprechen dem hohen Niveau aus Gymnasien in Bayern, die das

Schülerbuch Green Line New 4

im Unterricht verwenden und auf tatsächlich gestellten Aufgaben basieren.

Als Schüler kennst du ***Vocabulary*** mit Übungen zu Vokabeln und ***Grammar*** mit Übungen zur Grammatik. ***Speaking*** lernst du zum Training der Sprachfertigkeit. ***Writing*** übst du durch ***Dictation*** und schulst das Schreiben mit Diktatübungen. ***Dialogue*** und ***Mediation*** dient zur Übersetzung ins Englische. ***Reading Comprehension*** fördert das Textverständnis. ***Listening Comprehension*** verbessert das Hörverstehen.

Mit diesem Band kannst du Schritt für Schritt alle Schulaufgaben durcharbeiten, bis du fit bist für die nächste Schulaufgabe. Wenn der Lehrer eine Schulaufgabe ankündigt, sagt er z.B. von Unit 1 bis einschließlich Unit 2, dann solltest du die entsprechenden Schulaufgaben üben. Versuche die Aufgaben selbstständig zu lösen wie in einer richtigen Schulaufgabe. Gibt es einen Hörtext im Lösungsteil, lass dir den Text zweimal vorlesen. Vergleiche deine Lösungen mit den Lösungen der Schulaufgaben und korrigiere dich selbst. Wenn sich die Fehler häufen, dann musst du verstärkt Vokabeln lernen oder in der Grammatik oder im Schülerbuch noch einmal die Kapitel, um die es geht, wiederholen.

Mein Ziel ist es, die Motivation und Kreativität aller Schüler beim Lösen von Schulaufgaben in Englisch zu fördern. Dazu biete ich die **ausführliche Lösung** der Aufgabenstellung an.

Viel Spaß beim Lösen der Schulaufgaben

Deine und Ihre Englischtrainerin Monika Arndt

Monika Arndt (Dipl.-Übersetzerin), veröffentlichte als Buchautorin Ernährungsbücher für Kinder in den Verlagen dtv und Ravensburger. **Das Baby-Kochbuch**, **Wie Kinder fit und gesund bleiben** und **Das Ravensburger Kochbuch für Kinder** mit Bildern von Ali Mitgutsch.

Zuvor hat Monika Arndt in verschiedenen Redaktionen gearbeitet, z.B. über zehn Jahre in der Redaktion des Schulfernsehheftes beim Bayerischen Schulfernsehen. Beim Stark-Verlag hat sie über Produktion und Inhalt von Lernhilfen Erfahrungen gesammelt, geeignete Lehrer gesucht und die Bücher als Lektorin redigiert.

Sie unterrichtet Englisch und Französisch im ***Durchblicker Lernstudio Arndt***.

Wir danken Mike Cross, der diesen Band kritisch durchgesehen hat.

Titelbild: Heinrich Schmid, Überlingen am Ried / Singen am Hohentwiel

www.durchblicker.org

ISBN **978-3-00-036559-1**

9 783000 365591

1. Schulaufgabe aus dem Englischen

Name: ___________________________

Stoff: Unit 1–2

I. Reading Comprehension: Australia

Australia is a sweeping romantic adventure event film created by internationally celebrated and award winning writer, producer and director, Baz Luhrmann

Australia is an epic and romantic action adventure, set in that country just before the beginning of World War II[1]. In it, the English aristocrat Lady Sarah Ashley (Nicole Kidman) travels to the faraway continent where she meets the rough-hewn[2] local Drower (Hugh Jackman) and slowly and unwillingly agrees to join forces[3] with him to save the land that she had inherited[4]. Together, they go on a transforming[5] journey across hundreds of miles of the world's most beautiful but unforgiving terrain, only to face the bombing of the city of Darwin by the Japanese army that attacked Pearl Harbour. With his new film, Luhrmann is painting on a large canvas[6], creating a cinematic[7] experience that brings together romance, drama, adventure and spectacle.

Baz Luhrmann, the man who gave new life to the Hollywood musical with *Moulin Rouge*, has spent two years creating the biggest film ever made about Australia – a big film that tells a big story about a big country.

Filmed throughout the Northern Territory, Western Australia, New South Wales and Queensland, the land of Australia plays an important role in this fascinating work. Catherine Martin, the Production and Costume Designer, who won the Academy Award twice, brilliantly re-created the Australian outback and Darwin of the 1930s.

[1] World War II = der Zweite Weltkrieg, [2] A rough-hewn person is very simple and more or less wild.
[3] force = power, [4] to inherit = to get money, houses etc. from someone after they have died
[5] to transform = to completely change s.th., [6] canvas = Leinwand, [7] cinematic (adj.) cinema
[www.bigpondmovies.com/libraries/article_library/news/australia/synopsis_and_movie_background/abridged]

1. Questions on the text

Tick the correct answers. More than one answer can be correct. Do not tick off too many solutions for one question or you will not receive any credits for this question

Australia

A is a movie.
B was created by Nicole Kidman.
C is about a real story.
D plays in 1920.
E contains a lot of action.

The actors of *Australia* are

A Drower
B Martin
C Jackman
D Luhrmann
E Kidman
F Darwin
G Ashley

	right	wrong	not in the text
The author of the text says that Australia has a lot of beauty and dangers.	( )	( )	( )
Lady Sarah Ashley bought some land in Australia.	( )	( )	( )
The two heroes go to Darwin.	( )	( )	( )
They fall in love.	( )	( )	( )
Australia is the first film that Luhrmann created in Australia.	( )	( )	( )
The film plays in the 1930s.	( )	( )	( )
Martin's costumes are very different from those of the Australia of the 1930s.	( )	( )	( )

2. Language

What's the meaning of the underlined phrases?

1. She agrees <u>to join forces with him</u>.
   A She finally wants to work together with him.
   B She wants to fight against him.

2. They go on a <u>transforming</u> journey.
   A The country changes during the journey.
   B The heroes change during the journey.

3. With his new film, <u>Luhrmann is painting on a large canvas</u>.
   A Luhrmann is a painter.
   B Luhrmann's film is as colourful as a picture.

II. Grammar and Vocabulary: The fate[8] of Australia's Aborigines

1. Fill in the gaps: Put in the missing word. When there is a (+) the word is <u>not</u> in the box! Use one word from the box when there is a (*) and translate it
Put the verbs in brackets into the correct tense and aspect – active or passive. Use past perfect when possible

heiraten * Krankheiten * Regierungs- * Gesetz * grausam * Siedlungen* die gleichen Rechte* wahrscheinlich

The first people came to Australia from southeast ________Asia________(+) between 35,000 and 60,000 years ago. At the time of the British ____________________ (*), about 300,000 Aboriginal people were living in Australia. Europeans ________________ (to think) of their new colony as terra nullis – a land that ________________ (to own) by nobody – so many of the Aboriginal people ________________________ (to force) from their traditional lands and thousands __________________ (to kill). A great number__________________(to die) of ________________________ (*) that the white settlers __________________ (to bring) with them. In the first part of the 20th century, the Aboriginal people still ______________________ (not to have) ______________________ (*) as the whites. They could even not decide where __________________ (to live) or who they should _____________________ (*), for example. By the _____________________ (*) of the Australian __________________ (*) agents and church missions were allowed to remove children from their Aboriginal mother if it was ____________________ (*) that the father was not an Aborigine. The parents could not decide on the future of their children. This __________________ (*) practice ___________________ (to end) in the 1970s. Before this time, agents and church missions _____________________ (to take) away thousands of Aboriginal children from their families for years. At least 35,000 children, who are sometimes called the "_________________________" (+), were removed from their parents. Since 1998, the Australian people _______________________ (to change) their opinion about their dark past: A national Sorry Day __________________________ (to celebrate) every year on May 26. On February 12, 2008 a formal apology[9] ___________________ (to give) by Prime Minister Kevin Rudd, but a lot of Aboriginal people ______________________ (not to be able) so far to forget their terrible past.

[8] fate = Schicksal
[9] formal apology = offizielle Entschuldigung

2. Translate the following sentences into English

a) Anna begab sich ins Paradies.

____

b) Du kannst nicht durch den Tunnel fahren, es sei denn du hast ein Ticket.

____

____

c) Ich sollte lieber eine Menge Essen mitnehmen, denn entlang des Weges gibt es keinen Laden. (Benutze nicht I should und lots of food!)

____

____

____

III. Text Production

Meet the Millers

Word Chain: Use the following words in the box to write a short story on a day in the life of the Millers. Include each word and write about 180-200 words

warmer Sommer Tag * die Millers * die Burtons * Grillen * Hühnchen * Benny, der Hund * hungrig * Hühnchen weg! * Pizza * "Schau mal, was Benny macht!"

Good luck !

Lösung: 1. Schulaufgabe aus dem Englischen

I. Reading Comprehension: Australia

Australia is a sweeping romantic adventure event film created by internationally celebrated and award winning writer, producer and director, Baz Luhrmann

Australia is an epic and romantic action adventure, set in that country just before the beginning of World War II[1]. In it, the English aristocrat Lady Sarah Ashley (Nicole Kidman) travels to the faraway continent where she meets the rough-hewn[2] local Drower (Hugh Jackman) and slowly and unwillingly agrees to join forces[3] with him to save the land that she had inherited[4]. Together, they go on a transforming[5] journey across hundreds of miles of the world's most beautiful but unforgiving terrain, only to face the bombing of the city of Darwin by the Japanese army that attacked Pearl Harbour. With his new film, Luhrmann is painting on a large canvas[6], creating a cinematic[7] experience that brings together romance, drama, adventure and spectacle.

Baz Luhrmann, the man who gave new life to the Hollywood musical with *Moulin Rouge*, has spent two years creating the biggest film ever made about Australia – a big film that tells a big story about a big country. Filmed throughout the Northern Territory, Western Australia, New South Wales and Queensland, the land of Australia plays an important role in this fascinating work. Catherine Martin, the Production and Costume Designer, who won the Academy Award twice, brilliantly re-created the Australian outback and Darwin of the 1930s.

[www.bigpondmovies.com/libraries/article_library/news/australia/synopsis_and_movie_background/, abridged]

1. Questions on the text

Tick the correct answers. More than one answer can be correct. Do not tick off too many solutions for one question or you will not receive any credits for this question

Australia	x	A	is a movie.
		B	was created by Nicole Kidman.
		C	is about a real story.
		D	plays in 1920.
	x	E	contains a lot of action.
The actors of *Australia* are		A	Drower
		B	Martin
	x	C	Jackman
		D	Luhrmann
	x	E	Kidman
		F	Darwin
		G	Ashley

Statement	right	wrong	not in text
The author of the text says that Australia has a lot of beauty and dangers.	(x)	( )	( )
Lady Sarah Ashley bought some land in Australia.	( )	(x)	( )
The two heroes go to Darwin.	(x)	( )	( )
They fall in love.	( )	( )	(x)
Australia is the first film that Luhrmann created in Australia.	( )	( )	(x)
The film plays in the 1930s.	(x)	( )	( )
Martin's costumes are very different from those of the Australia of the 1930s.	( )	(x)	( )

2. Language

What's the meaning of the underlined phrases?

1. She agrees to join forces with him.
   - A *x* She finally wants to work together with him.
   - B She wants to fight against him.

2. They go on a transforming journey.
   - A The country changes during the journey.
   - B *x* The heroes change during the journey.

3. With his new film, Luhrmann is painting on a large canvas.
   - A Luhrmann is a painter.
   - B *x* Luhrmann's film is as colourful as a picture.

____/21

II. Grammar and Vocabulary: The fate[8] of Australia's Aborigines

1. Fill in the gaps: Put in the missing word when there is a (+). It is not in the box!
Use one word from the box when there is a (*) and translate it
Put the verbs in brackets into the correct tense and aspect – active or passive. Use past perfect when possible

heiraten * Krankheiten * Gesetz * Regierung * grausam * Siedlungen* die gleichen Rechte* wahrscheinlich *(get married * illness * law * government * cruel * settlements * the same rights * likely to)*

The first people came to Australia from southeast *Asia* (+) between 35,000 and 60,000 years ago. At the time of the British *settlements* (*), about 300,000 Aboriginal people were living in Australia. Europeans *thought* (to think) of their new colony as terra nullis – a land that *had been owned* (to own) by nobody – so many of the Aboriginal people *were forced* (to force) from their traditional lands and thousands *were killed* (to kill). A great number *died* (to die) of *illness* (*) that the white settlers *had brought* (to bring) with them. In the first part of the 20th century, the Aboriginal people still *didn't have* (not to have) *the same rights* (*) as the whites. They even could not decide where *to live* (to live) or who they should *get married to* (*), for example. By the *law* (*) of the Australian *government* (*) agents and church missions were allowed to remove children from their Aboriginal mother if it was *likely* (*) that the father was not an Aborigine. The parents could not decide on the future of their children. This *cruel* (*) practice *ended* (to end) in the 1970s. Before this time, agents and church missions *took* (to take) away thousands of Aboriginal children from their families for years. At least 35,000 children, who are sometimes called the "*stolen generation*" (+), were removed from their parents. Since 1998, the Australian people *have been changing* (to change) their opinion about their dark past: A national Sorry Day *has been celebrated* (to celebrate) every year on May 26. On February 12, 2008 a formal apology *was given* (to give) by Prime Minister Kevin Rudd, but a lot of Aboriginal people *haven't been able* (not to be able) so far to forget their terrible past. ____/27

[8] fate = Schicksal
[9] formal apology = offizielle Entschuldigung

Tipps und Hinweise
Das **Passiv** besteht aus einer Form von ***to be + Past Participle***. Wenn der Urheber der Handlung nicht wichtig ist, verwendet man das Passiv. Dann wird das Objekt des Aktivsatzes zum Subjekt des Passivsatzes. Bei zwei Objekten wird meist das Dativobjekt (indirektes Objekt) gebraucht. Das direkte Objekt (Akkusativobjekt) wird nur verwendet, wenn es hervorgehoben wird. Präpositionen bleiben immer beim Verb. Der Handelnde wird nur genannt, wenn es zusätzliche Informationen gibt.

2. Translate the following sentences into English

a) Anna begab sich ins Paradies.

Anna made her way to paradise.

b) Du kannst nicht durch den Tunnel fahren, es sei denn du hast ein Ticket.

You can't drive through the tunnel unless you have a ticket.

c) Ich sollte lieber eine Menge Essen mitnehmen. Entlang des Weges gibt es keinen Laden.
(Benutze nicht I should und lots of food!)

I'd better take plenty of food. There are no shops along the way.

III. Text Production

Meet the Millers

Word Chain: Use the following words in the box to write a short story on a day in the life of the Millers. Include each word and write about 180-200 words

warmer Sommer Tag * die Millers * die Burtons * Grillen * Hühnchen * Benny, der Hund * hungrig * Hühnchen weg! * Pizza * "Schau mal, was Benny macht!"

warm summer day * the Millers * the Burtons * barbecue * chicken * Benny, the dog * hungry * chicken is gone * pizza * "Look, what Benny's doing!"

On a great, warm day in summer the Millers decided to invite the Burtons for a barbecue. Mrs Miller was making some sausages and sandwiches while Mr Burton made a huge chicken, that was hard work! After that they put glasses on the table and started to grill the chicken. But what was Benny, their dog, doing? A few minutes later the Burtons arrived and the two families started to great each other. However, the Burtons were very hungry – they hadn't eaten anything since breakfast. So they all went immidiately to barbecue. But what was that? The chicken was gone, just like the sausages and the sandwiches. Mr Miller was very embarassed but he didn't want the Burtons to go home. He proposed to go to a pizzeria to buy a pizza for everybody. Anyway, the pizzas tasted good but everybody had been looking forward to barbecue. Suddenly Bobby Burton shouted: "Look, what Benny's doing!" Benny was sitting behind a bush while he was eating something! There they were: the chicken, the sausages. "Oh, Benny," Mrs Miller laughed, "have you been so hungry?" ____/20

Total ____/68

1. Schulaufgabe aus dem Englischen

Name: ____________________________

Stoff: Unit 1–2

I. Listening Comprehension *(Text aus Lösung 2x vorlesen lassen)*

Listen to the following text twice. Answer the questions afterwards

[1]breeding = Brut

Questions on the text

Answer the following questions. Sometimes more than one answer is correct. Be sure to tick all the correct answers but do not tick too many or you won't get the full points

1. Australia is …
   - ___ the smallest country in the world..
   - ___ the smallest continent in the world.
   - ___ 21 times smaller than Germany.
   - ___ 21 times the size of Germany.
   - ___ a city in England.

2. The Aborigines…
   - ___ make up a majority of Australians.
   - ___ were the first animals in Australia.
   - ___ were the first humans in Australia.
   - ___ do not exist anymore.
   - ___ are a tourist attraction.

Statement	true	false	not in the text
Australia is a tourist attraction.	( )	( )	( )
Kangaroos, monkeys and koalas all live in Australia.	( )	( )	( )
Lake Eyre is 15 meters above sea level.	( )	( )	( )
The Aborigines came to Australia over 5.000 years ago.	( )	( )	( )
Sydney is a city in Australia.	( )	( )	( )
Lake Eyre is good for the breeding events for hens.	( )	( )	( )
Australia is a movie.	( )	( )	( )
Australia is bordering the Pacific Ocean.	( )	( )	( )
Australian English is easy to understand.	( )	( )	( )
Winter in Australia is from July until August.	( )	( )	( )

II. Vocabulary

1. Explain these words in English. Use complete sentences

a) settler: ______________________________

b) to depend (on) sb: ______________________________

c) silence: ______________________________

2. Translate these sentences into English

a) Akzeptiere keine Widerrede!

____

b) Er wird wahrscheinlich mit roten Schuhen kommen.

____

c) Zu ihrem Besten musste sie eine kurze Hose und ein T-Shirt anziehen.

____

III. Indirect speech

Lin and Matt finally met at the beach to go surfing and they were having a short conversation. Read through their conversation and then *report to your friend what Lin and Matt were talking about*. Make sure that you use different introductory verbs with every sentence and also mind the indirect commands Matt gives Lin

Matt: Hey Lin, it's nice that you've found time to go surfing with me. We can try this new trick today!

He said that it was nice that she had found time to went surfing with him. He said that they could try his new trick that day.

Lin: OK, but I have to be careful because I haven't done any surfing for two years now. Things were really crazy before we moved here.

Matt: Was it hard for you to leave all your friends?

Lin: I really miss all of them but I'm glad that I met you last week and that you invited me to go surfing.

Matt: I'm sure that we will have a lot of fun together. But please be careful. And look out for sharks; there might be some here this time of the year.

Lin: Ok, but Matt, don't forget to put sun lotion on before we start!

IV. Grammar

If-clauses: Fill in the missing forms in the if-clauses and the main clauses of the sentences. Make sure that you use the correct conditional types!

Lin and Matt had a lot of fun surfing that day. After one hour Lin could do the new trick Matt had told her about perfectly. If Matt didn't show (not show) her how to do it, she wouldn't learn (not learn) it so fast. He tried to motivate her, when he said: "I will buy (buy) you some ice cream later if you are able (be able) to show me that jump perfectly at the end of the day." But when they swam out into the deeper water for the first time Lin suddenly pointed at a shark flipper[1]. Matt ________ (not see) the shark if Lin ________ (not shout) so loudly. They turned around immediately and swam back to the beach. Lin breathed heavily and said: "I ________ (cry) right now if you ________ (not be) here to comfort[2] me." "That's what friends do. I ________ (always be) there for you if you ________ (be) in trouble." They sat at the beach and watched the flipper for some time. "I ________ (teach) you that new jump if we ________ (to be able to go) back out there." Matt whispered. "We ________ (get bitten) by the shark if we ________ (go) back into the water!" Lin replied. While sitting and watching the flipper Lin and Matt could see that it was just a fake flipper on the head of a child. They started laughing and ran back into the water. "I ________ (tell) the boy that that was not a good joke if I ________ (see) him later!" Matt shouted. "I ________ (tell) him right now if I ________ (not have) something much better to do!" Lin replied and laughed out loud. "Let's do that new trick of yours." They ________ (miss) a wonderful day if they ________ (leave) the beach straight away.

[1]flipper: Flosse
[2]to comfort somebody: jemanden beruhigen

V. Text Production: A letter

While you are spending your holidays in Australia with your friend Alexandra Weiß, you are writing a letter to your best friend at home and telling him / her what different things you have experienced and what important places of Australia you have already seen. Give three examples and make sure that you have a suitable beginning and ending for your letter (130 words)

Use these first four lines to take notes. They won't be corrected or marked.

____

____

____

____

(Use an extra sheet of paper)

Good luck !

Lösung: 1. Schulaufgabe aus dem Englischen

I. Listening Comprehension *(Text 2x vorlesen lassen)*

Listen to the following text twice. Answer the questions afterwards

The first humans to live in Australia were the Aborigines. It is known that the first Aborigines immigrated to Australia over 50.000 years ago from Asia. Up to this day there are Aborigines living in Australia but it is rarely that a tourist can see them. They want to keep to themselves and do not want to be a tourist attraction.

Australia is the smallest continent but 21 times the size of Germany. The land is relatively flat. The seasons in Australia are the opposite from the northern hemisphere. Australia's summer is from December until February and their wintertime is from June to August. The North can have tropical temperatures and there is a rain season from November until April. Even if one has great English skills, understanding Australians' will be a challenge. The Australian slang differs especially in the choice of words and pronunciation from British and American English. Therefore it is oftentimes hard to understand native Australians.

In Australia's forests you can find a lot of eucalyptus trees. Animals such as the kangaroo, koala or emu are what Australia is famous for. There are street signs announcing these animals.

Australia borders the Indian Ocean and the Pacific Ocean. Lake Eyre is Australia's lowest point at about 15 meters below sea level. It only rarely fills with water and usually has a number of sub lakes. In good years the lake can fill and if it does it is a great living area for birds. This is because it then supports major breeding[1] events of birds for example the Australian Pelican.

Questions on the text

Answer the following questions. Sometimes more than one answer is correct. Be sure to tick all the correct answers but do not tick too many or you won't get the full points.

1. Australia is …

___ the smallest country in the world.
_x_ the smallest continent in the world.
___ 21 times smaller than Germany.
_x_ 21 times the size of Germany.
___ a city in England.

2. The Aborigines…

___ make up a majority of Australians.
___ were the first animals in Australia.
_x_ were the first humans in Australia.
___ do not exist anymore.
___ are a tourist attraction.

Statement	true	false	not in text
Australia is a tourist attraction	( )	(x)	( )
Kangaroos, monkeys and koalas all live in Australia.	( )	(x)	( )
Lake Eyre is 15 meters above sea level.	( )	(x)	( )
The Aborigines came to Australia over 5.000 years ago.	( )	(x)	( )
Sydney is a city in Australia.	( )	( )	(x)
Lake Eyre is good for the breeding events for hens.	( )	(x)	( )
Australia is a movie.	( )	( )	(x)
Australia is bordering the Pacific Ocean.	(x)	( )	( )
Australian English is easy to understand.	( )	(x)	( )
Winter in Australia is from July until August.	( )	(x)	( )

____/ 20

II. Vocabulary

1. Explain these words in English. Use complete sentences

a) settler: *A person who comes to a new country and lives there, making it a new home.*

b) to depend (on) sb: *To rely and trust someone.*

c) silence: *When there is no sound and it is absolutely quiet.*

____/3

2. Translate these sentences into English

a) Akzeptiere keine Widerrede!

Don't take no for an answer.

b) Er wird wahrscheinlich mit roten Schuhen kommen.

He is likely to come in red shoes.

c) Zu ihrem Besten musste sie eine kurze Hose und ein T-Shirt anziehen.

In her best interest she had to wear shorts and a t-shirt.

____/3

III. Indirect speech

Lin and Matt finally met at the beach to go surfing and they were having a short conversation. Read through their conversation and then *report to your friend what Lin and Matt were talking about.* Make sure that you use different introductory verbs with every sentence and also mind the indirect commands Matt gives Lin

Matt: Hey Lin, it's nice that you've found time to go surfing with me. We can try this new trick today!

He told her that it was nice that she had found time to go surfing with him and that they could try that new trick that day.

Lin: OK, but I have to be careful because I haven't done any surfing in two years now. Things were really crazy before we moved here.

She warned him that she had to be careful because she hadn't done any surfing in two years. She explained that things had been really crazy before they had moved there.

Matt: Was it hard for you to leave all your friends?

He asked her whether it had been hard for her to leave all her friends.

Lin: I really miss all of them but I'm glad that I met you last week and that you invited me to go surfing.

She answered that she really missed all of them but she was glad that she had met him the week before and that he had invited her to go surfing.

Matt: I'm sure that we will have a lot of fun together. But please be careful. And look out for sharks; there might be some here this time of a year.

He said that he was sure that they would have a lot of fun together and advised her to be careful. He reminded her to look out for sharks. There might be some there that time of the year.

Lin: And you don't forget to put sun lotion on before we start!

She wanted him not to forget to put sun lotion on before they started.

____/20

Tipps und Hinweise
Verschiedene ***Introductory verbs*** sind z.B. ***say, tell, explain, mention, point out, ask, reply, agree, disagree, shout, yell, scream, cry.***
Bei der **indirekten Rede** musst du darauf achten, dass aus Orts- bzw. Zeitangaben wie ***here*** oder ***this time of the year*** in der direkten Rede, ***there*** bzw. ***that time of the year*** geformt wird. Die Angaben werden an die Person angepasst.
Steht das Verb in der **direkten Rede** im ***Simple Past*** oder ***Past Perfect*** musst du darauf achten, dass du die Verbform in der **indirekten Rede** um eine Zeitstufe in die Vergangenheit **zurück** setzt, z.B. wird ***will →would   is → was   start → started***
Achtung auch, wenn in der **direkten Rede** eine **Frage** ohne Fragewort verwendet wird! Hier musst du in der **indirekten Rede** die Frage durch ***if*** oder ***whether*** einleiten.

IV. Grammar

If-clauses: Fill in the missing forms in the if-clauses and the main clauses of the sentences. Make sure that you use the correct conditional types!

Lin and Matt had a lot of fun surfing that day. After one hour Lin could do the new trick Matt had told her about perfectly. If Matt *hadn't shown* (not show) her how to do it, she *wouldn't have learned* (not learn) it so fast. He tried to motivate her, when he said: "I *will buy* (buy) you some ice cream later if you *are able* (be able) to show me that jump perfectly at the end of the day." But when they swam out into the deeper water for the first time Lin suddenly pointed at a shark flipper[1]. Matt *wouldn't have seen* (not see) the shark if Lin *hadn't shouted* (not shout) so loudly. They turned around immediately and swam back to the beach. Lin breathed heavily and said: "I *would cry* (cry) right now if you *weren't* (not be) here to comfort[2] me." "That's what friends do. I *will always be* (always be) there for you if you *are* (be) in trouble." They sat at the beach and watched the flipper for some time. "I *would teach* (teach) you that new jump if we *were able to go* (to be able to go) back out there." Matt whispered. "We *will get bitten* (get bitten) by the shark if we *go* (go) back into the water!" Lin replied. While sitting and watching the flipper Lin and Matt could see that it was just a fake flipper on the head of a child. They started laughing and ran back into the water. "I *will tell* (tell) the boy that it was not a good joke if I *see* (see) him later!" Matt shouted. "I *would tell* (tell) him right now if I *didn't have* (not have) something much better to do!" Lin replied and laughed out loud. "Let's do that new trick of yours." They *would have missed* (miss) a wonderful day if they *had left* (leave) the beach straight away.

____/20

Tipps und Hinweise
Bei den **if-Sätzen** gibt es drei verschiedene Typen:
Typ I: Der if-clause scheint eine **erfüllbare Bedingung** zu sein, der main clause eine **Folge für die Zukunft**. Im if-clause wird das ***Simple Present*** verwendet, im main clause ***will future*** (oft auch Hilfsverben: *can, must, needn't, ...*) oder der Imperativ.
Typ II: Der if-clause scheint eine **nur theoretisch oder gar nicht erfüllbare Bedingung** zu sein, der main clause eine **Folge für Zukunft oder Gegenwart.** Im if-clause wird das ***Simple Past*** verwendet, im main clause das ***Conditional (would + infinitive form)***.
Typ III: Der if-clause ist eine **nicht mehr erfüllbare Bedingung.** Der main clause die **immer noch wirksame Folge**. Im if-clause wird das ***Past Perfect*** verwendet, im main clause das ***Conditional Perfect (would + have + past participle)***.

V. Text production: A letter

While you are spending your holidays in Australia with your friend Alexandra Weiß, you are writing a letter to your best friend at home and tell him / her what different things you have experienced and what important places of Australia you have already seen. Give three examples and make sure that you have a suitable beginnning and ending for your letter (130 words)

Harbour Bridge, opera, Great Barrier Reef, outback, kangaroo, Aborigines

Dear Mona,

I am fine. It is really nice here in Australia and Alexandra and I have had a lot of fun. Last week we were scuba diving at the Great Barrier Reef. There were a lot of interesting things and animals like corals, white sharks which kill one person in Australia each year and cute dolphins. We climbed Harbour Bridge where we had a fantastic view over a big part of Sydney, the largest city of Australia. We made a sightseeing tour around the famous opera. Yesterday, we took a trip to the outback where we saw lots of animals like kangaroos; they are dangerous because they can cause car accidents. In rivers and lakes there are saltwater crocodiles, the largest reptile on earth. Never try swimming where signs forbid you to, or local people say it's not save. Normally the local people know what animals to watch out for. The Aborigines are the native inhabitants of Australia. I'll tell you more about them when I'm back.

See you soon. Bye ... ____/30

Total ____/96

Tipps und Hinweise
Briefe kann man mit ***Dear…, My dear…, Hello…, Hi…*** beginnen.
Mögliche **Endungen** sind z.B. ***See you soon, Bye, Yours…, Love…, Best wishes***

2. Schulaufgabe aus dem Englischen

Name: ______________________________

Stoff: Unit 2–3, Focus 1

I. Facts about Scotland

Alain, your exchange student from France wants to travel to Scotland. He remembers that you learned something about Scotland in your English lesson while he was here but he couldn't understand everything, so he asks you a few questions. Can you help him? Write your answer in complete sentences

a) Alain: "I read that you had to see the Military Tattoo? What's that?"

You: ____

____

____

b) Alain: "I see. What do you know about Nessie?"

You: ____

____

____

c) Alain: "A lot of Scottish names start with "Mac". What does "Mac" mean?

You: ____

____

____

d) Alain: "What's the name of the skirt the musicians wear?"

You: ____

____

____

e) Alain: "What else do you know about the funny skirt?"

You: ____

____

____

II. Vocabulary

1. Alain copied what was written on the blackboard but he spilled some water on his paper and now he can't read some of the words anymore. Can you help him by filling in the gaps?

Christopher Columbus was a very ____________________________ (having knowledge and skill from doing things) sailor. He knew how to sail around _______________________ (high area of land with a very steep side, usually near the sea) and he could steer his ship into small bays, so called _________________________ . He even _____________________ a new continent, America. He actually wanted to find a new route to _______________________ for the Spanish queen in 1492. Ships and navigation had been improved so people were able to _____________________ regions that had been unknown before. At that time it was very dangerous to sail the seas because there were many pirates robbing __________________ (the goods a ship is carrying – e.g. wine, tobacco, ...). If pirates were caught, they were ___________________ (another word for "to kill in order to punish"). If a ship hit a rock, it sank and often its crew __________________ because they were not able to swim. The dead bodies sank to the _________________ of the sea.

____ / 10

2. Alain heared the teacher say something about "orphanage" and "inherit" but he didn't know what these words meant – explain the words to him – write complete sentences

a) orphanage:

____

____

____

____

b) to inherit:

____

____

____

____

III. Grammar

1. Rewrite the sentences below. Write down all possible passive forms (personal passive and passive if possible)

a) Before we met our French exchange student, the people from the exchange program Alain is with had sent us a brochure about the city Alain comes from.

b) The first day at school I will introduce Alain to my friends at school.

c) "You should show Alain the school building."

d) I explained all the rules to Alain.

2. Correct the mistakes Alain has made with the definite and indefinites articles

Back in the France, Alain wrote you letter telling you what he did week before: Alain and his friend Max interviewed pupils at the school. Two afternoons in the week they stood in hall after the lunch for a half hour and talked to people who went by. They wanted to know what the boys and girls argued about the most with their parents. For the most of them a quick answer was quite the problem. Many said that the pocket money was big problem as was the coming home late. They had both expected the answers to be something like this. Especially coming home late was one of things they most discussed in their families. But it was new that helping in a house or having an much older boyfriend were also mentioned quite an often. Almost nobody argued about the school.

3. Fill in the gaps with the correct verb forms and correct pronouns

Alain: "Do you think my new trousers ____________ (to suit) me? Do you think I should buy ____________ (it / them)?"

You : "I'm not so sure. I think the best advice ____________ (to come) from the shop assistants. Let's ask them."

Alain: "Excuse me, I need help with ____________ (this /these) trousers. 150 Euros ____________ (to sound) too much, don't you think?"

Shop assistant : "Well, the clothes we sell here ____________ (to be) really expensive. Why don't you have a look at the jeans we sell upstairs? They are much cheaper there."

Alain: "Great, thank you! Where ____________ (to be) the stairs?

Shop assistant : "Over there!"

Alain to you: "The German people ____________ (to be able to) speak English properly."

IV. Text Production

Alain is very interested in history
1. He wants to know why the Elizabethan Age (the time when Queen Elizabeth I was queen) is often called the Golden Age
2. Explain what changes there were during her reign. Write about 100 words

Good luck !

Lösung: 2. Schulaufgabe aus dem Englischen

I. Facts about Scotland

Alain, your exchange student from France wants to travel to Scotland. He remembers that you learned something about Scotland in your English lesson while he was here but he couldn't understand a lot, so he asks you a few questions. Can you help him? Write your answer in complete sentences

a) Alain: "I read that you had to see the Military Tattoo? What's that?"

You: *It's the most popular shows at the Edinburgh Festival. It's also a big international celebration.*

b) Alain: "I see. What do you know about Nessie?"

You: *Nessie is something like a legend here in Scotland. People say she's a monster that lives in Loch Ness. Especially tourists believe in Nessie and want to buy souvenirs of her.*

c) Alain: "A lot of Scottish names start with "Mac". What does "Mac" mean?

You: *Mac usually stands in front of Scottish names. Mac Alister for example means that it is the son of the old Mac Alister.*

d) Alain: "What's the name of the skirt the musicians wear?"

You: *It's called a kilt.*

e) Alain: "What else do you know about the funny skirt?"

You: *Actually the kilt was invented in England. It's the traditional clothes of the Scotts. Every family has its own tartan – that's the colour and pattern of the cloth.*

____/8

II. Vocabulary

1. Alain copied what was written on the blackboard but he spilled some water on his paper and now he can't read some of the words anymore. Can you help him by filling in the gaps?

Christopher Columbus was a very *experienced* (having knowledge and skill from doing things) sailor. He knew how to sail around *cliffs* (high area of land with a very steep side, usually near the sea) and he could steer his ship into small bays, so called *coves*. He even *discovered* a new continent, America. He actually wanted to find a new route to *India* for the Spanish queen in 1492. Ships and navigation had been improved so people were able to *explore* regions that had been unknown before. At that time it was very dangerous to sail the seas because there were many pirates robbing *cargo* (the goods a ship is carrying – e.g. wine, tobacco, ...). If pirates were caught, they were *executed* (another word for "to kill in order to punish"). If a ship hit a rock, it sank and often its crew *drowned* because they were not able to swim. The dead bodies sank to the *bottom* of the sea.

____/10

2. Alain heared the teacher say something about "orphanage" and "inherit" but he didn't know what these words meant – explain the words to him – write complete sentences

a) orphanage:

Children whose parents are dead or whose parents don't take care of them are often sent to orphanages where they're looked after by other people.

b) to inherit:

If your parents die you'll probably inherit the possessions that they owned before their death.

____/4

III. Grammar

1. Rewrite the sentences. Write down all possible passive forms (personal passive and passive if possible)

a) Before we met our French exchange student, the people from the exchange program Alain is with had sent us a brochure about the city Alain comes from.

We had been sent a brochure about the city Alain comes from by the exchange program.

A brochure about the city Alain comes from had been sent to us by the exchange program.

b) The first day at school I will introduce Alain to my friends at school.

Alain will be introduced to my friends.

c) "You should show Alain the school building."

Alain should be shown the school building.

The school building should be shown to him.

d) I explained all the rules to Alain.

All the rules were explained to him.

____/8

Tipps und Hinweise
Personal Passive: beim Übersetzen ins Deutsche werden häufig Sätze mit ‚man´ oder ‚jemand´ verwendet.
Passiv 2: Das indirekte Objekt wird mit to angeschlossen (häufig eine Person).

2. Correct the mistakes he has made with the definite and indefinites articles

Back in France, Alain wrote you a letter telling you what he did the week before: Alain and his friend Max interviewed pupils at school. Two afternoons in a week they stood in the hall after lunch for half an hour and talked to the people who went by. They wanted to know what the boys and girls argued about most with their parents. For most of them a quick answer was quite a problem. Many said that pocket money was a big problem as was coming home late. They had both expected the answers to be something like this. Especially the coming home late was one of the things they most discussed in their families. But it was new that helping in the house or having a much older boyfriend were also mentioned quite often. Almost nobody argued about school.

____/10

Tipps und Hinweise
Der **unbestimmte Artikel** wird meist wie im Deutschen gebraucht. Ausnahmen: Bei Nationalitätsangaben oder Berufsbezeichnungen, einzelnen Wörtern wie z.B. *half, quite, rather, such,* bei Zeit- und Mengenangaben sowie in bestimmten Redewendungen (z.B. *in a hurry*).
Der **bestimmte Artikel** wird verwendet, wenn Nomen näher bestimmt sind (z.B. durch Orts- oder Zeitangaben oder einen Relativsatz), eine bestimmte Institution (das Gebäude davon) gemeint ist, oder Familiennamen im Plural stehen.
Es wird **kein Artikel** verwendet, wenn man an den Zweck einer Institution denkt (Schule: Unterricht, Kirche: Gottesdienst, Bank: Geldgeschäfte), wenn Stoffbezeichnungen, unzählbare Begriffe, Verkehrsmittel, Monate, Wochentage oder Mahlzeiten allgemein verwendet werden und bei Personennamen im Singular.

3. Fill in the gaps with the correct verb forms and correct pronouns

Alain: "Do you think my new trousers *suit* (to suit) me? Do you think I should buy *them* (it / them)?"

You : "I'm not so sure. I think the best advice *comes* (to come) from the shop assistants. Let's ask them."

Alain: "Excuse me, I need help with *these* (this /these) trousers. 150 Pounds *sounds* (to sound) too much, don't you think?"

Shop assistant : "Well, the clothes we sell here *are* (to be) really expensive. Why don't you have a look at the jeans we sell upstairs? They are much cheaper there."

Alain: "Great, thank you! Where *are* (to be) the stairs?

Shop assistant : "Over there!"

Alain: "The German people *are able to* (to be able to) speak English properly." ____/8

Tipps und Hinweise
Manche Paarwörter wie **trousers** (→ zwei Hosenbeine) werden im Englischen mit **pluralistischer Bedeutung** gesehen. Deshalb werden sie nur im Plural verwendet.
Auch **clothes** und **stairs** werden **nur im Plural** verwendet.
Gruppenbezeichnungen wie **people** haben im Englischen auch ausschließlich **pluralistische Bedeutung**.

IV. Text Production

Alain is very interested in history
1. He wants to know why the Elizabethan Age (the time when Queen Elizabeth I was queen) is often called the Golden Age
2. Explain what changes there were during her reign. Write about 100 words

Dear Alain,

I hope you're fine. This is the reply to the letter you wrote to me last week.

These are the facts you have to known about the Elizabethan Age which is also called the Golden Age. England was very powerful. When Queen Elizabeth I. ruled the country, it was a period of time when Great Britain became really rich, which is why the Elizabethan Age is also called the Golden Age.

Printing wasn't possible at all, before the printing press was invented. First Gutenberg invented the printing press. Later when the Reformation had started it helped Luther who had translated the bible into German. It was also the time when England and Spain made many sailing trips to explore other countries and found new colonies. Drama also wasn't very popular during that time. One of the most famous playwriter was William Shakespeare.

If you've got any questions now, you can write me an e-mail.

____/20

Total ____/68

2. Schulaufgabe aus dem Englischen

Name: ___________________________

Stoff: Unit 3–4

I. Reading Comprehension

Read the following text carefully

The Highland Games

In Scotland there are events to celebrate the Scottish and Celtic heritage and culture throughout the year. One of them is the Highland Games. In the 11th century[1] King Malcom III, then king of Scotland organised the Highland Games to find the strongest and fastest men in his country. Back then the fastest men became the king's new couriers[2] and the strongest men his bodyguards. Now the Games have competitions in bag piping, drumming and dancing and also some athletics[3]. It is a tradition for the Scottish families to have someone participate[4] in the Games. The Games are also taking place in other countries where Scotts have settled. Today's games attract many visitors. The British Royal Family even attends the events in Braemar. Braemar is where King Malcom III used to have his events back in the 11th century. One of the games is the caber toss[5]. A caber is a 5 metres long log[6], which weights about 45 kg. The athlete holds the carber by one end and then tries to throw it away so it lands on the other end and falls away from the thrower[7]. Other games are for example hammer throw or rope pulling. The atmosphere at the Highland Games is wonderful and you can learn about Scotland, it's history and meet Scottish people.

[1] century = Jahrhundert
[2] couriers = Kuriere
[3] athletics = Sport
[4] participate = teilnehmen
[5] caber toss = Baumstammwurf
[6] log = Holzstamm
[7] thrower = person who throws sth

Questions on the text

1. According to the text, are these statements true, false or not answered in the text? Mark your answer with an x

Statement	true?	false?	not in text
In the 11th century the strongest men became the kings new courirs.			
The Highland Games are only held in Scotland.			
Today's Highland Games are also a festival of dance and music.			

2. Complete the following sentences according to the text. Mark the right answers with an x

a) Malcom III

___ is long and heavy.
___ lives in Braemar now.
___ was a Scottish king.
___ is also a contest for bag pipers.
___ is an athlete.

b) A cabar

___ is long and heavy.
___ lives in Braemar now.
___ was a Scottish king.
___ is also a contest for bag pipers.
___ is an athlete.

c) At the Highland Games, there

___ lives in Braemar now.
___ was a Scottish king.
___ is also a contest for bag pipers.
___ is an athlete.

II. Vocabulary

1. Explain these words in English. Use complete sentences

a) permanent: ____

____

____

b) to blame: ____

____

____

c) wimp: ____

____

____

d) to call s.b. names: ____

____

____

2. Fill in the word that is described

a) If you plan to do something in the future with someone else, this plan is called

______________________ .

b) You ______________________ something is true, if you think it is but don't really know for sure.

c) If you express something in a different way but that the meaning stays the same you

______________________ it.

3. Give the opposite to the word (one word answer)

a) ugly ⇔ ______________________

b) to shake your head ⇔ ______________________

c) a coward ⇔ ______________________

III. Grammar

1. Sue is going on a trip to Scotland with her class. She is very excited and telling her friend about the upcoming trip in a letter
Sue forgot to put in all the articles. Can you help her by filling them in the blanks? Use the definite, indefinite or no article

Dear Hanna,

I am going on _____ trip to _____ Scotland. I am sure ____ time I spend there will be great. I really like ____ history and I am especially interested in ____ history of Scotland. I think that ____ history is ____ really important subject. Usually I don't like ____ trips but I am sure ____ trip to Scotland will be fun. My whole ____ class is going. It will take seven hours to get to Edinburgh by ____ train and then ____ hour to get to our ____ hotel. I am looking forward to ____ trip and will send you ____ postcard from Scotland.

I hope to get ____ letter from you soon!

Love, Sue

2. Translate the sentences into English, please. Be careful with the singular and plural of nouns

a) Das Hochlandvieh sieht sehr schön aus. Ich war überrascht was es kostet.

____

____

b) Die Nachrichten kommen im Fernsehen (TV). Sie sind sehr interessant.

____

____

c) Ich habe meine Sonnenbrille vergessen! Jetzt scheint die Sonne, also brauche ich sie.

____

____

d) Als wir zur Schule kamen hat die Polizei uns Fragen gefragt.

____

____

e) Vergiss deine Schere nicht. Wir brauchen sie später.

____

____

IV. Text Production

Imagine you are on a trip with your school. You are attending the Highland Games in Braemar with your class. You're writing a postcard to your friend in England telling him / her about what you experience. Write the postcard. Write about 100 words

Good luck !

Lösung: 2. Schulaufgabe aus dem Englischen

I. Reading Comprehension

Read the following text carefully

The Highland Games

In Scotland there are events to celebrate the Scottish and Celtic heritage and culture throughout the year. One of them is the Highland Games. In the 11th century[1] King Malcom III, then king of Scotland organised the Highland Games to find the strongest and fastest men in his country. Back then the fastest men became the king's new couriers[2] and the strongest men his bodyguards. Now the Games have competitions in bag piping, drumming and dancing and also some athletics[3]. It is a tradition for the Scottish families to have someone participate[4] in the Games. The Games are also taking place in other countries where Scotts have settled. Today's games attract many visitors. The British Royal Family even attends the events in Braemar. Braemar is where King Malcom III used to have his events back in the 11th century. One of the games is the caber toss[5]. A caber is a 5 metres long log[6], which weights about 45 kg. The athlete holds the carber by one end and then tries to throw it away so it lands on the other end and falls away from the thrower[7]. Other games are for example hammer throw or rope pulling. The atmosphere at the Highland Games is wonderful and you can learn about Scotland, it's history and meet Scottish people.

Questions on the text

1. According to the text, are these statements true, false or not answered in the text? Mark your answer with an x

Statement	**true?**	**false?**	**not in text**
In the 11th century the strongest men became the kings new courirs.		x	
The Highland Games are only held in Scotland.		x	
Today's Highland Games are also a festival of dance and music.	x		

____/3

2. Complete the following sentences according to the text
Mark the right answers with an x

a) Malcom III

___ is long and heavy.
___ lives in Braemar now.
_x_ was a Scottish king.
___ is also a contest for bag pipers.
___ is an athlete.

b) A caber

_x_ is long and heavy.
___ lives in Braemar now.
___ was a Scottish king.
___ is also a contest for bag pipers.
___ is an athlete.

c) At the Highland Games, there

___ is long and heavy.
___ lives in Braemar now.
___ was a Scottish king.
_x_ is also a contest for bag pipers.
___ is an athlete.

____/3

II. Vocabulary

1. Explain these words in English. Use complete sentences

a) permanent: *Something that is there for a very long time or forever is permanent.*

b) to blame sb: *To blame somebody means saying that it is their fault.*

c) wimp: *A wimp is somebody who is weak and too afraid to do things that might be difficult or dangerous.*

d) to call sb names: *To call somebody names means someone is using nasty words to describe somebody.*

____/8

> **Tipps und Hinweise**
>
> Achtung: Pass auf! Blamieren und **to blame** sind *false friends!*

2. Fill in the word that is described

a) If you plan to do something in the future with someone else, this plan is called *arrangement*.

b) You *guess* something is true, if you think it is but don't really know for sure.

c) If you express something in a different way but that the meaning stays the same you *paraphrase* it.

____/3

3. Give the opposite to the word (one word answer)

a) beautiful ⇔ *ugly*

b) to shake your head ⇔ *to nod*

c) a coward ⇔ *a hero*

____/3

II. Grammar

1. Sue is going on a trip to Scotland with her class. She is very excited and telling her friend about the upcoming trip in a letter
Sue forgot to put in all the articles. Can you help her by filling them in the blanks? Use the definite, indefinite or no article

Dear Hanna,

I am going on *a* trip to Scotland. I am sure *the* time I spend there will be great. I really like history and I am especially interested in *the* history of Scotland. I think that history is *a* really important subject. Usually I don't like trips but I am sure *the* trip to Scotland will be fun. My whole class is going. It will take seven hours to get to Edinburgh by train and then *an* hour to get to our *the* hotel. I am looking forward to *the* trip and will send you *a* postcard from Scotland.

I hope to get *a* letter from you soon!

Love, Sue

____/16

Tipps und Hinweise
Der **unbestimmte Artikel** wird meist wie im Deutschen gebraucht. Ausnahmen: Bei Nationalitätsangaben oder Berufsbezeichnungen, einzelnen Wörtern wie z.B. *half, quite, rather, such,* bei Zeit- und Mengenangaben sowie in bestimmten Redewendungen (z.B. *in a hurry*).
Der **bestimmte Artikel** wird verwendet, wenn Nomen näher bestimmt sind (z.B. durch Orts- oder Zeitangaben oder einen Relativsatz), eine bestimmte Institution (das Gebäude davon) gemeint ist, oder Familiennamen im Plural stehen.
Es wird **kein Artikel** verwendet, wenn man an den Zweck einer Institution denkt (Schule: Unterricht, Kirche: Gottesdienst, Bank: Geldgeschäfte), wenn Stoffbezeichnungen, unzählbare Begriffe, Verkehrsmittel, Monate, Wochentage oder Mahlzeiten allgemein verwendet werden und bei Personennamen im Singular.

2. Translate the sentences into English, please
Be careful with the singular and plural of nouns

a) Das Hochlandvieh sieht sehr schön aus. Ich war überrascht was es kostet.

Highland Cattle look very beautiful. I was surprised what they cost.

b) Die Nachrichten kommen im Fernsehen (TV). Sie sind sehr interessant.

The news is on TV. It is very interesting.

c) Ich habe meine Sonnenbrille vergessen! Jetzt scheint die Sonne, also brauche ich sie.

I forgot my sunglasses! Now the sun is shining and I need them.

d) Als wir zur Schule kamen, hat die Polizei uns Fragen gestellt.

When we got to school the police asked us questions.

e) Vergiss deine Schere nicht. Wir brauchen sie später.

Don't forget your scissors. We will need them later. ____/10

Tipps und Hinweise
Cattle und ***police*** werden immer als Gruppe gesehen. Sie stehen deshalb immer mit den **Pluralformen** von Verben und Pronomen.
Sunglasses und ***scissors*** sind Dinge, die aus zwei Teilen bestehen. Sie werden im Englischen auch immer im **Plural** verwendet.
Manche Nomen haben die Pluralendung -s (wie z.B. ***news***), werden aber als eine Einheit gesehen und deshalb wie eine **Singularform** verwendet.

IV. Text Production

Imagine you are on a trip with your school. You are attending the Highland Games in Braemar with your class. You're writing a postcard to your friend Anna in England telling him / her about your experience. Write the postcard

Dear Anna,

I am on a trip to Scotland with my class. We attended some festival in Braemar. It is called the Highland Games. There was lots of music and dance at the festival. Most of the Scottish people here were wearing the traditional clothes. They wore a kilt and some of them play the bag pipes. There were some contests in bag piping and also in dance. There were also some athletic games. One of them is called carber toss. I think the atmosphere was great and we had a lot of fun. I really like Scotland and the people here are nice.

Love, Chris

____/20

Total ____/66

1. Schulaufgabe aus dem Englischen

Name: ____________________________

Stoff: Unit 5–6

I. Reading Comprehension

The Freedom Trail is a 2,5-mile path (= 4 km) in Boston, which contains 16 sites[1] (leading back to the Revolutionary War)

You can take a guided tour or make your own by looking at the map on the Trail's[2] website. A red path on the ground marks the Trail. Different things can be explored while taking the path. You can find out how people lived in the 1770s at Paul Revere's house, which he purchased[3] in 1770. King's Chapel shows what the church was like. Right next to the chapel is the King's Chapel Burying Ground. Here Mary Chilton, the first woman who stepped off the Mayflower is buried[4]. The Faneuil Hall Marketplace is like other shopping centres in America, full of food courts[5] and stores. You come across the Boston Common, which is America's oldest public park. The end of the Revolutionary War was once celebrated here with big fireworks. The Old Corner Bookstore was once a pharmacy[6] in 1711 and only later in 1828 a bookstore was opened here. The USS Constitution is the oldest commissioned[7] warship. On the ship you can take a tour, see how the crew[8] lived. In the captains room a diary is exposed with the words "The war is over". The Freedom Trail is a great opportunity to find out about the history of the Revolutionary War. It is an indoor-outdoor museum that attracts many tourists each year.

[1] sites = Sehenswürdigkeiten / Stätten
[2] Trail = Fußweg
[3] to purchase = to buy
[4] buried = beerdigt
[5] food courts = Gastronomiebereich
[6] pharmacy = Apotheke
[7] commissioned = beauftragt
[8] crew = soldiers who work on the ship

Questions on the text

Tick the correct answers. More than one answer can be correct. Do not tick off too many solutions for one question or you will not receive any credits for this question

1. The Freedom Trail is

A an indoor museum.
B a museum in the USA.
C a path that leads to different sites.
D located in Boston.
E purchased by Paul Revere.

2. The USS Constitution is

A the ship, Mary Chilton was on.
B a warship during World War II.
C a site on the Freedom Trail.
D the newest commissioned warship.
E ruled by the king.

Statement	true	false	not in text
1. Paul Revere bought a pharmacy in 1770.	( )	( )	( )
2. The Faneuil Marketplace is a food court.	( )	( )	( )
3. The USS Constitutions had a captain.	( )	( )	( )
4. Mary Chilton was the first woman to step off the Mayflower.	( )	( )	( )
5. The Freedom Trail is on the history of the Revolutionary War.	( )	( )	( )
6. The Captain's diary says "World War II is over".	( )	( )	( )
7. Some of the crew members of the USS Constitution were killed during the war.	( )	( )	( )

II. Vocabulary

1. Explain these words in English. Use complete sentences

a) shy: ____

____

b) to enclose: ____

____

c) to be crazy about: ____

____

d) tough: ____

____

2. Give two possible explanations of each of the words in English. Write in complete sentences

a) pretty: → ____

____

____

→ ____

____

____

b) to burst: → ____

____

____

→ ____

____

____

II. Grammar

1. Fill in the missing words. If there is no word in brackets think about what is the correct form to put in. Watch out for the gerund and infinitive forms

Dear Sue,

I hope you are ______________ well. I was ______________ (sprechen) to Peter yesterday when Josh came up and asked me ______________ (gehen) to the dance with him. I can't imagine ________________ with Josh. He is nice but I like Peter more. Peter said he wouldn't mind __________________ to the dance with someone else. I didn't know what __________________ (sagen). The dance is the party __________________ (gehen) to if you're cool, so I really want ____________________. I decided __________________ "no" to Josh because _______________ with Peter is more fun, I think. I mean, I would like

____________ with both of them but that is not possible.

Today Josh walked past me without __________________ a word. I can't stand Josh

____________ (sein) upset with me, but I guess he will be for a while. There is no need for

him _______________ angry.

What are you ________________ about all this? Are you still thinking of _______________

to Munich for the weekend of the dance? I hope you are. I really want you _______________

here.

I am looking forward to ________________ from you soon.

Anne

2. Translate the following sentences into English. Be careful with the infinitive and gerund forms

a) Schwimmen ist gut für deine Fitness.

____

____

b) Er hat Angst alleine zu gehen.

____

____

c) Er brachte sie dazu "nein" zu sagen.

____

____

d) Ich kann viel riskieren.

____

____

e) Die Polizei hatte Probleme den Entführer zu verhaften.

____

____

IV. Text Production

Imagine you are a police officer. You are working in London, England and want to write a letter to your friend in Ireland. You want to tell him / her about your last workday. Write the letter. Use the words in the box. Write about 120-140 words

Lösegeld * entführen * riskieren * Gefahr * sorgen * Tresor * Polizei * Telefon

Good luck !

Lösung: 1. Schulaufgabe aus dem Englischen

I. Reading Comprehension

The Freedom Trail is a 2,5-mile path (= 4 km) in Boston, which contains 16 sites[1] (leading back to the Revolutionary War)

You can take a guided tour or make your own by looking at the map on the Trail's[2] website. A red path on the ground marks the Trail. Different things can be explored while taking the path. You can find out how people lived in the 1770s at Paul Revere's house, which he purchased[3] in 1770. King's Chapel shows what the church was like. Right next to the chapel is the King's Chapel Burying Ground. Here Mary Chilton, the first woman who stepped off the Mayflower is buried[4]. The Faneuil Hall Marketplace is like other shopping centres in America, full of food courts[5] and stores. You come across the Boston Common, which is America's oldest public park. The end of the Revolutionary War was once celebrated here with big fireworks. The Old Corner Bookstore was once a pharmacy[6] in 1711 and only later in 1828 a bookstore was opened here. The USS Constitution is the oldest commissioned[7] warship. On the ship you can take a tour, see how the crew[8] lived. In the captains room a diary is exposed with the words "The war is over". The Freedom Trail is a great opportunity to find out about the history of the Revolutionary War. It is an indoor-outdoor museum that attracts many tourists each year.

Questions on the text

Tick the correct answers. More than one answer can be correct. Do not tick off too many solutions for one question or you will not receive any credits for this question

1. The Freedom Trail is

	A	an indoor museum.
	B	a museum in the USA
x	C	a path that leads to different sites.
x	D	located in Boston.
	E	purchased by Paul Revere.

2. The USS Constitution is

	A	the ship, Mary Chilton was on.
	B	a warship during World War II.
x	C	a site on the Freedom Trail.
	D	the newest commissioned warship.
	E	ruled by the King.

Statement	true	false	not in text
Paul Revere bought a pharmacy in 1770.	( )	(x)	( )
The Faneuil Marketplace is a food court.	( )	(x)	( )
The USS Constitutions had a captain.	(x)	( )	( )
Mary Chilton was the first woman to step off the Mayflower.	(x)	( )	( )
The Freedom Trail is on the history of the Revolutionary War.	(x)	( )	( )
The Captain's diary says "World War II is over".	( )	(x)	( )
The USS Constitution is bigger than the Mayflower.	( )	( )	(x)
Some of the crew members of the USS Constitution were killed during the war.	( )	( )	(x)

____/18

II. Vocabulary

1. Explain these words in English. Use complete sentences

a) shy: *Someone who is shy does not say a lot and often feels nervous when he / she is together with other people.*

b) to enclose: *If you enclose something in a letter you put something in with the letter you want to send.*

c) to be crazy about sth: *Someone who is crazy about something likes it very, very much.*

d) tough: *Something that is tough for you is really hard for you to do.*

____/4

2. Give two possible explanations of each of the words in English. Write in complete sentences

a) pretty: → *A person that looks good is pretty.*

→ *If something is pretty good, it is really good.*

b) to burst: → *When something bursts, it suddenly breaks open (example: a balloon can burst suddenly).*

→ *When you burst into a room, you come in really suddenly. Or: When you burst into a laugh, you suddenly start laughing.*

____/4

III. Grammar

1. Fill in the missing words. If there is no word in brackets think about what is the correct form to put in. Watch out for the gerund and infinitive forms

Dear Sue,

I hope you are *doing* well. I was *talking* (sprechen) to Peter yesterday when Josh came up and asked me *to go* (gehen) to the dance with him. I can't imagine *dancing* with Josh. He is nice but I like Peter more. Peter said he wouldn't mind *going* (gehen) to the dance with someone else.

I didn't know what *to say* (sagen). The dance is the party *to go* to if you're cool, so I really want *to be* there. I decided *to say* "no" to Josh because *going* with Peter is more fun, I think.

I mean, I would like *to stay* with both of them but that is not possible.

Today Josh walked past me without *saying* a word. I can't stand Josh *being* (sein) upset with me, but I guess he will be for a while. There is no need for him *to be* angry.

What are you *thinking* about all this? Are you still thinking of *coming* to Munich for the weekend of the dance? I hope you are. I really want you *to be* here.

I am looking forward to *hearing* from you soon.

Anne

____/18

2. Translate the following sentences into English. Be careful with the infinitive and gerund forms

a) Schwimmen ist gut für deine Fitness.

Swimming is good for your fitness.

b) Er hat Angst alleine zu gehen.

He was afraid of going alone. Or: He was afraid of going by himself.

c) Er brachte sie dazu "nein" zu sagen.

He made her say "no".

d) Ich kann viel riskieren.

I can risk a lot.

e) Die Polizei hatte Probleme den Entführer zu verhaften.

The police had problems / trouble arresting the kidnapper.

____/10

Tipps und Hinweise
Das **Gerund** wird als Substantiv, das von einem Verb abgeleitet ist verwendet (substantiviertes Verb). Es steht nach bestimmten **Adjektiven mit Präpositionen** z.B. ***be afraid of, be bad / good at*** ; nach bestimmten **Präpositionen** wie z.B. ***before, after***; nach bestimmten **Verben** z.B. ***enjoy, love, keep, prefer, start***; nach bestimmten **Verben mit Präposition** z.B. ***look forward to, think about, talk about*** und nach bestimmten **Nomen mit Präpositionen** z.B. ***a chance of, a way of.***

Der **Infinitiv mit to** wird nach bestimmten Verben z.B. ***decide***, nach Verb + Objekt z.B. ***want***; nach Fragewörtern z.B. ***what***; nach Nomen z.B. ***place***. Außerdem steht er nach ***the first, the last, the only*** und nach der Konstruktion: **Adjektiv / Nomen + for + Nomen / Pronomen.**

IV. Text Production

Imagine you are a police officer. You are working in London, England and want to write a letter to your friend in Ireland. You want to tell him / her about your last workday. Write the letter. Use the words in the box. Write about 120-140 words (Use an extra sheet of paper)

Lösegeld * entführen * riskieren * Gefahr * sorgen * Tresor * Polizei * Telefon

Dear Frank,

I have to tell you about a day last week. I was working as usual at the police office when suddenly the phone rang. A man screamed into the phone, telling me that a stranger kidnapped his wife. He said that the kidnapper wanted ransom in order to set his wife free. He was worrying a lot and wanted me to help. I asked him where he was and immediately drove to his place. We could find out where the kidnapper kept his wife and I went there. It was a few blocks away. I had to put myself into a lot of danger and almost risked my life because the kidnapper had a gun. I could safe the wife though and found a safe with lots of money in it.

____/16

Total ____/70

3. Schulaufgabe aus dem Englischen

Name: ______________________________

Stoff: Unit 5–6

I. Listening Comprehension *(Text aus Lösung 2x vorlesen lassen)*

Listen to the following text twice. Answer the questions afterwards

Questions on the text

Answer the following questions. Sometimes more than one answer is correct. Be sure to tick all the correct answers but do not tick too many or you won't get the full points.

1. Commissar Hunter…
   ___ was having a coffee break when a lady came in the office.
   ___ was filling out forms when a lady came in.
   ___ was working the late night shift.
   ___ was amused by what the lady looked like.
   ___ tried to steal the pistol.

2. Commissar Pete…
   ___ came by the office on accident.
   ___ knew immediately what was going on.
   ___ was one of Commisar Hunter's colleagues.
   ___ wanted to help.
   ___ laughed when he saw the lady's coat.

3. The lady…
   ___ was screaming.
   ___ was hurt.
   ___ knew Commissar Pete.
   ___ knew Commissar Hunter.
   ___ wanted help.

Statement	true	false	not in text
Commissar Hunter yelled at the lady to be quiet.	( )	( )	( )
The lady shot her husband.	( )	( )	( )
Commissar Pete saw when the husband got shot.	( )	( )	( )
The lady's husband was a criminal.	( )	( )	( )
The husband was a doctor.	( )	( )	( )
Commissar Pete took the train to work.	( )	( )	( )
Commissar Hunter took the pistol from the lady.	( )	( )	( )
The lady was wearing Jeans and a T-shirt.	( )	( )	( )
There was blood on the lady's clothes.	( )	( )	( )
Commissar Hunter caught the criminal.	( )	( )	( )

II. Vocabulary

Translate the following sentences into English

a) Anscheinend war er der Unterhaltungskünstler bei der Party der Präsidentin.

____

____

b) Zum Glück hat sich Lea um mich gekümmert.

____

____

c) Ermutigende Worte geben dir Zuversicht.

____

____

III. Grammar

1. Complete the following sentences by putting the words in the brackets into the correct form!

1. Do you enjoy ____________________ (read) detective stories, or would you like ____________________ (be) a private detective yourself?

2. If you are interested in the adventures of Sherlock Holmes and his confidant Dr. Watson, the Sherlock Holmes Museum in 221B Baker Street is definitely the place ______________ (visit).

3. Although London is famous for ____________ (be) one of the biggest cities in the word, the museum is quite easy _____________ (find) because there are so many signs _________________ (show) you the right way.

4. Instead of _____________________ (waste) your time in a pub or in one of London's shopping malls, it is absolutely worth ________________ (spend) a couple of hours there in order _____________ (see) at least the most fascinating exhibits.

5. Step back in time, and whenever you are in London, remember ________________ (visit) the world's most famous address!

2. Translate these sentences into English. Watch out for the adverbial forms. Use the words in brackets

1. Das Essen war gut genug (enough) und es gab genug davon.

____

____

2. Sollen wir uns heute Abend am Kino treffen?

____

____

3. Ich muss immer aufräumen und Lisa muss nie.

____

____

III. Creative Writing

Read the following introduction and write down how the story continues. Write about 120 words

William had a letter in his hand. Time was running out, he had to get to the post office as quickly as possible. This was his last chance....

Good luck !

Lösung: 3. Schulaufgabe aus dem Englischen

I. Listening Comprehension *(Text 2x vorlesen lassen)*

Listen to the following text twice. Answer the questions afterwards

Commissar Hunter was sitting at his office desk when suddenly a lady came into the police office. “Help, help, help”, she screamed. Commissar Hunter looked up. What was going on? “How can I help you?”, he asked. “My husband! My husband! You have to come. I need your help commissar! He shot him in the leg. I saw it. I saw his pistol. Come. Get him. The murderer”, the lady screamed. “Calm down, Mrs. And please, start from the beginning. What happened”. Commissar Hunter tried to calm the lady down. “I don’t have time to calm down, sir. I need your help! How can you just sit there? He shot him. My husband only tried to help. I don’t want that criminal to just get by with what he did!” Commissar Hunter put away the forms he was filling out and went over to the counter. He looked at the lady and didn’t know how to calm her down. The lady was wearing her nightgown and over it a long thick coat. He now noticed she was holding a pistol in her hands. She was shaking and her eyes were wide open. Commissar Hunter asked the lady to please sit down. He got a glass of water and gave it to her. At the same time he said, “Can you please hand me that pistol”. He took the pistol out of her hand and put it down on his desk. The lady was going on about how the murderer had shot her husband. Suddenly his colleague Commissar Pete came in the room. He saw the pistol and the lady and noticed some bloodstains on her coat. He turned to Hunter and asked, “What is going on here? What’s the matter?” Hunter told his colleague quickly what the lady had said so far. Commissar Pete thought to himself “I wonder if she is talking about the man that was taken away with an ambulance just a few minutes ago right outside the train station?” Pete had just started his shift at the police office and usually took the train to work. That’s how he saw the crazy fight right outside the train station. He thought he had seen a lady with a long coat just like hers but why was she holding the pistol that was missing at the crime scene? This was mysterious.

Questions on the text

Answer the following questions. Sometimes more than one answer is correct. Be sure to tick all the correct answers but do not tick too many or you won't get the full points

1. Commissar Hunter…

___ was having a coffee break when a lady came in the office.
_X_ was filling out forms when a lady came in.
___ was working the late night shift.
___ was amused by what the lady looked like.
___ tired to steal the pistol

2. Commissar Pete…

___ came by the office on accident.
___ knew immediately what was going on.
_X_ was one of Commisar Hunter's colleagues.
___ wanted to help.
___ laughed when he saw the lady's coat.

3. The lady…

_X_ was screaming.
___ was hurt.
___ knew Commissar Pete.
___ knew Commissar Hunter.
_X_ wanted help.

Statement	**true**	**false**	**not in text**
Commissar Hunter yelled at the lady to be quiet.	( )	(x)	( )
The lady shot her husband.	( )	(x)	( )
Commissar Pete saw when the husband got shot.	( )	(x)	( )
The lady's husband was a criminal.	( )	(x)	( )
The husband was a doctor.	( )	( )	(x)
Commissar Pete took the train to work.	(x)	( )	( )
Commissar Hunter took the pistol from the lady.	(x)	( )	( )
The lady was wearing Jeans and a T-shirt.	( )	(x)	( )
There was blood on the lady's clothes.	(x)	( )	( )
Commissar Hunter caught the criminal.	( )	( )	(x)

____ /25

II. Vocabulary

Translate the following sentences into English

a) Anscheinend war er der Unterhaltungskünstler bei der Party der Präsidentin.

Apparently he was the entertainer at the president's party.

b) Zum Glück hat sich Lea um mich gekümmert.

Fortunately Lea took care of me.

c) Ermutigende Worte geben dir Zuversicht.

Encouraging words give you confidence.

____/8

III. Grammar

1. Complete the following sentences by putting the words in the brackets into the correct form!

1. Do you enjoy *reading* (read) detective stories, or would you like *to be* (be) a private detective yourself?
2. If you are interested in the adventures of Sherlock Holmes and his confidant Dr. Watson, the Sherlock Holmes Museum in 221B Baker Street is definitely the place *to visit* (visit).
3. Although London is famous for *being* (be) one of the biggest cities in the world, the museum is quite easy *to find* (find) because there are so many signs *to show* (show) you the right way.
4. Instead of *wasting* (waste) your time in a pub or in one of London's shopping malls, it is absolutely worth *spending* (spend) a couple of hours there in order *to see* (see) at least the most fascinating exhibits.
5. Step back in time, and whenever you are in London, remember *to visit* (visit) the world's most famous address!

____/10

Tipps und Hinweise

Das Gerund verhält sich wie ein Substantiv. Es wird nach folgenden Verben verwendet: ***admit, avoid, can't help, couldn't help, can't stand, complain about, consider, be crazy about, deny, detest, dislike, enjoy, excuse, finish, hate, imagine, insist on, keep (= continue), look forward to, mind, miss, practise, prevent, regret, resist, resume, risk, stand (= tolerate), stop, suggest.*** Nach feststehenden Ausdrücken: ***What about, how about, it's no use, it's no good, it's worth.*** Nach adverbialen Nebensätzen: ***On seeing, after noticing, instead of looking for, in spite of knowing, by getting, for being, being keen on going.***

Infinitiv mit to steht nach folgendem **Verb + Infinitiv**: ***afford, agree, arrange, begin, decide, forget, hesitate, hate, hope, learn, love, manage, offer, plan, promise, refuse, remember, seem, threaten, try.*** Example: *She promised to come.* Nach folgendem **Adjektiv + Infinitiv**: ***able, difficult, easy, glad, happy, likely, nice, pleased, possible, sad, sorry.*** Example: *It must be difficult to do that.* Nach folgendem **Substantiv + Infinitiv: ability, decision, wish.** Nach folgendem **Verb + Objekt + Infinitiv**: ***advise, ask, allow, beg, command, encourage, force, make, order, remind tell, warn, believe, consider, expect, hate, know, (would) like, love, promise, think, want.*** Example: *Mum told Jim to go swimming.*

2. Translate these sentences into English. Watch out for the adverbial forms Use the words in brackets

1. Das Essen war gut genug (enough) und es war genug davon übrig.

The food was good enough and there was enough of it left.

2. Sollen wir uns heute Abend am Kino treffen?

Should we meet at the cinema tonight?

3. Ich muss immer aufräumen und Lisa muss nie.

I always have to clean up and Lisa never has to.

____/7

Tipps und Hinweise

Adverbien der **Häufigkeit** wie z.B. ***always, sometimes, never, often*** stehen in der Regel entweder **zwischen** Subjekt und Vollverb oder Hilfsverb und Vollverb.
Adverbien der **Zeit** wie z.B. ***tomorrow, yesterday, for seven days*** stehen in der Regel meist **hinter** dem Vollverb (falls vorhanden Objekt). Manchmal stehen sie auch **vor** dem Subjekt.
Besonderheit bei *enough*: *enough* wird in der Regel **nach** gestellt, **außer** wenn es als **Mengenangabe** für ein Nomen gebraucht wird.

III. Creative Writing

Read the following introduction and write down how the story continues. Write about 120 words

William had a letter in his hand. Time was running out, he had to get to the post office as quickly as possible. This was his last chance....

The letter had to be sent off today in order to arrive at Laura's place before Tom. Tom was taking the train and William knew that once Tom saw Laura he would tell her.
William couldn't let that happen. He wanted to be the first to tell Laura. He wanted to tell her how much he loved her. William was afraid that Laura would marry Tom if he didn't write this letter. He wanted to admit his love. So William wrote. He wrote and wrote as if it meant saving a life. William told Laura that he loved her so and that he could not imagine living without her. He ran to the post office and made it just in time.

____/20

Tipps und Hinweise

Das **Passiv** besteht aus einer Form von ***to be + Past Participle***. Wenn der Urheber der Handlung nicht wichtig ist, verwendet man das Passiv. Dann wird das Objekt des Aktivsatzes zum Subjekt des Passivsatzes. Bei zwei Objekten wird meist das Dativobjekt **(indirektes Objekt)** gebraucht. Das **direkte Objekt** (Akkusativobjekt) wird nur verwendet, wenn es hervorgehoben wird. Präpositionen bleiben immer beim Verb. Der Handelnde wird nur genannt, wenn es zusätzliche Informationen gibt.

Total ____/ 70

Monika und Claus Arndt aus Waldtrudering geben im Eigenverlag Lernhilfen für Schüler heraus

Die Durchblick-Garanten

Die Tage sind gezählt bis zu den Sommerferien. Nicht alle Schüler jedoch tun sechs Wochen lang nichts für die Schule. Und es gibt so einige Eltern, die sich jetzt schon fürs neue Schuljahr rüsten. Viele von ihnen landen bei Monika und Claus Arndt aus Waldtrudering. Das Ehepaar gibt Hefte mit Schulproben für Grundschüler und Schulaufgaben für Gymnasiasten und Realschüler heraus. Kinder und Jugendliche können sich mit ihren Durchblicker-Aufgaben auf Prüfungen vorbereiten.

Monika und Claus Arndt im Keller ihres Waldtruderinger Hauses. Dort drucken sie ihre Durchblicker-Schulaufgaben. Jahrelang haben sie zudem Nachhilfeunterricht gegeben, mittlerweile konzentrieren sie sich auf ihr Verlagsgeschäft. Ihre Schulaufgaben sind im Buchhandel zu finden und helfen Schülern bei der Lösung von Schulaufgaben. ***Fotos: Panthermedia/ve/kn***

Im Keller der Familie Arndt im Birkhahnweg in Waldtrudering läuft der Drucker. In den Regalen stapeln sich ordentlich die Ausdrucke. Ihre Bestellungen erreichen Monika und Claus Arndt meist spät abends. Nach Ladenschluss schicken Buchhändler noch ihre Bestellliste ab, so auch an den Durchblicker Verlag in Waldtrudering. Viele Jahre lang haben die Arndts im Keller Schülern Nachhilfeunterricht gegeben. Vor fünf Jahren haben sie einen Verlag gegründet und verkaufen seitdem Bücher mit typischen Schulaufgaben für bayerische Schüler. Derzeit, kurz vor den Sommerferien und vor allem dann im September, sei die Nachfrage besonders groß. „Wir haben ein saisonales Geschäft", sagt Claus Arndt schmunzelnd. Bevor es in die Ferien geht oder zum Start ins neue Schuljahr, bestellen Schüler und ihre Eltern die Durchblicker-Schulaufgaben.

Der Mathematiker sattelte aufs Lehramt um

Die Arndts haben sozusagen eine Marktlücke entdeckt: Verlage bieten zwar immer mehr Lernhilfen für Schüler an. Doch die Arndts haben ihre Ausgaben auf die jeweiligen Schultypen und auf die neuen Lehrpläne in Bayern zugeschnitten. So läuft und läuft ihr Drucker. „Volltreffer!", hat ihnen ein Schüler geschrieben, „drei Aufgaben in meiner Schulaufgabe waren genau wie die aus Ihrem Buch!" Und eine Buchhändlerin lässt sie wissen: „Ich empfehle die Reihe immer weiter. Sie haben in mir einen Fan gefunden."
Wie aber kommt es, dass die beiden Waldtruderinger so einen guten Riecher haben, wie Lehrer ihre Schulaufgaben gestalten und was sie wollen? Claus Arndt war als Diplom-Mathematiker in der EDV-Branche beschäftigt. Bis 2004. Da hieß es: „Wer gehen wolle, könne gehen." Der Waldtruderinger Vater zweier Söhne ließ sich das nicht zwei Mal sagen. Händeringend wurde damals nach Lehrern gesucht. So sattelte der Mathematiker kurzerhand um und unterrichtete fortan an der Realschule in Dachau und am Neuperlacher Heinrich-Heine-Gymnasium Mathe.
Damit nicht genug. Zuhause im Keller eröffnete er mit seiner Frau Monika ein Lernstudio für Schüler. Claus Arndt gab Nachhilfe in Mathematik. Seine Frau in Englisch, Deutsch und Französisch. „Für Physik und Latein beschäftigten wir noch weitere Nachhilfelehrer", erzählt Claus Arndt. Die Waldtruderinger Familien nahmen das Angebot gerne an: Bei den Arndts gab es Nachhilfe für den Achtklässler, der darum kämpfte, wegen Mathe bloß nicht durchzufallen. Ein anderer Bub, ein Grundschüler, konnte partout nicht stillsitzen. „Ich ließ ihn hier unten auf einem kleinen Trampolin auf- und abspringen und fragte ihn dabei das Einmaleins ab", erzählt Claus Arndt. Ebenso ackerten gleich mehrere Schüler in einem Crashkurs, um in ihrer Abschlussprüfung eine bessere Note zu bekommen.

Nachhilfeunterricht von 13 bis 20 Uhr

Vier Jahre lang büffelten die Nachhilfelehrer mit ihren Schützlingen Stunde für Stunde im Keller. „Unseren Höhepunkt hatten wir im Jahr 2008, da saßen wir von 13 bis 20 Uhr in unserem Lernstudio, die Nachfrage in Waldtrudering und Umgebung war einfach so groß", erinnert sich Claus Arndt. Was ist das Arndtsche Erfolgsrezept? Die Arndts lösen mit ihren Schülern Schulaufgaben, erarbeiten Musterlösungen und korrigieren die Antworten gemeinsam. „Diese Klassenarbeiten denken wir uns selbst aus", sagt Claus Arndt. Im Laufe der Jahre haben sie ein Gespür dafür entwickelt, welche Aufgabentypen drankommen können — „wie die Lehrer ticken".
Schulaufgaben zu entwickeln, das machte Claus Arndt bald nicht nur für seine Nachhilfeschüler im Münchner Osten. Für die Verlage Klett und Cornelsen modifizierte er Schulaufgaben. „Doch die Lehrpläne variieren von Bundesland zu Bundesland", erzählt der Klausuren-Profi. Und so schlug man ihm vor, für Bayern einfach selbst Schulaufgaben herauszugeben. Im Eigenverlag.
Claus Arndt hatte ja mit seiner Frau Monika kompetente Hilfe an seiner Seite. Denn vor allem sie war es, die in ganz Bayern Buchhändler abklapperte, um Werbung für die Durchblicker-Schulaufgaben zu machen. Mehr noch: Monika Arndt hatte als Autorin bereits Ernährungsbücher für Kinder veröffentlicht, hatte unter anderem beim Stark-Verlag über Produktion sowie Inhalt von Lernhilfen viele Erfahrungen gesammelt und als Lektorin gearbeitet. Sie knöpfte sich nun die Fächer Deutsch, Französisch und Englisch vor und arbeitete ebenso Schulaufgaben aus. Zudem sei es für sie als Schulaufgaben-Entwickler mit Einführung des G8 leichter geworden: „Alles ist systematischer und strukturierter, ich kann eher abschätzen, was in einer Klassenarbeit drankommt", sagt Claus Arndt.

Neu im Angebot sind Proben für Grundschüler

Mittlerweile haben sie eine breite Palette mit 57 verschiedenen Ausgaben im Angebot: Ob für Gymnasiasten Mathe-Schulaufgaben von der fünften bis hoch zur zwölften Klasse oder für Realschüler Englisch-Schulaufgaben. „Und neu und sehr beliebt sind unsere Schulproben in Mathe, Deutsch und HSU für Dritt- und Viertklässler", sagt Monika Arndt. „Die sind immer mehr unsere Renner!" Als Verlag profitieren sie von dem wachsendem Druck, der schon auf Grundschüler ausgeübt werde. „Eltern wollen unbedingt, dass ihr Kind einen Notendurchschnitt von 2,33 beim Übertrittszeugnis in der vierten Klasse hat, damit es aufs Gymnasium gehen kann", sagt Claus Arndt. „Das ist oft zu viel des Guten." Er weiß, wovon er spricht. Er hat in all den Jahren in seinem Lernstudio viele Kinder kennengelernt. „Oft haben wir gemerkt, welch großen Druck Eltern auf ihr Kind ausüben können." Natürlich müsse sich jedes Kind auf Tests in der Schule vorbereiten. Doch als Eltern zweier Söhne, 1993 und 1996 geboren, wissen sie eben auch, dass ein Kind nicht zu viel lernen dürfe. „Wer für eine Schulaufgabe mit zwei unserer Aufgaben übt, dem reicht das meist", behauptet Monika Arndt.
Den beiden Schulaufgaben- und Nachhilfe-Profis geht es vor allem darum, Schüler besser auf das vorzubereiten, was sie bei einer Probe erwartet. „Angst und Nervosität legen sich schnell, wenn Schüler ähnliche Aufgaben kennen und bereits bearbeitet haben", sagt Claus Arndt.

Verena Rudolf

Telefon (089) 53 06-420
lokales@merkur.de
Telefax: (089) 53 06-86 56

Mehr Durchblick für Schüler

Claus und Monika Arndt produzieren Lernhefte im heimischen Keller in Waldtrudering

VON LAURA MÜLLER

Vielen Kindern graut es vor der Schule. Häufig sind sie unmotiviert und wissen nicht, wie sie sich auf Tests und Schularbeiten vorbereiten sollen. Für diese Problematik gibt es eine Menge Nachhilfelehrer und Bücher, die helfen sollen. Einer der Verlage, die solche Bücher, oder vielmehr Hefte, produzieren, ist der Durchblicker Verlag – ein kleiner Buchverlag, der nur aus dem Ehepaar Claus und Monika Arndt besteht. Er hat sich auf Schulaufgaben und ihre Lösungen spezialisiert. Die Arndts produzieren die Hefte im heimischen Keller in Waldtrudering.

Die Nachfrage ist groß: Im Keller von Monika und Claus Arndt stapeln sich die Lernhefte des heimischen Verlags. Alles ist handproduziert, das ist das Markenzeichen des Verlags.

FOTOS: ASTRID SCHMIDHUBER

Auf den jungen Schülern lastet eine Menge Druck, sagen die Arndts

Claus Arndt, ein ehemaliger Software-Ingenieur, hat den Verlag vor fünf Jahren gegründet. Angefangen hat alles damit, dass Claus Arndt anfing, Nachhilfe zu geben. „Als die Kinder kamen, wollte ich nicht ständig unterwegs sein", erzählte er. „Also habe ich meinen Job gekündigt und Nachhilfe gegeben." Die Schüler kamen gerne zu Claus Arndt, so wurde die Nachfrage irgendwann zu groß. Die Arndts gaben das Lernbüro auf und fingen an, Bücher mit Schulaufgaben und ihren Lösungen zu drucken. Zunächst verkauften sie nur wenige Hefte, doch im vergangenen Jahr waren es schon 20000. Insgesamt haben sie 58 Bücher verfasst und herausgebracht. Die Arndts sehen sich mittlerweile als „ernst zu nehmende Konkurrenz" für den renommierten Stark-Verlag. Dessen rote Übungsbücher stehen bei vielen Schülern im Regal.

Claus Arndt sammelt seit der Umstellung auf das G8 Schulaufgaben von verschiedenen Schulen. Weil er selbst mal als Lehrer arbeitete, weiß er, was andere Lehrer erwarten. Claus und Monika Arndt orientieren sich bei ihren Aufgaben immer an dem neusten Stand der Lehrpläne.

Die Hefte des Durchblicker-Verlags: Insgesamt 58 Lerntrainer haben die Arndts schon herausgebracht.

Als die Arndts ihren Verlag gründeten, klapperten sie alle möglichen Büchereien ab, um ihre Bücher präsentieren zu können. Monika Arndt hat schon vorher als Lektorin und Autorin gearbeitet. Sie kennt sich in der Branche aus und weiß, wie man hier etwas erreicht. Heute liegen die Bücher des Durchblicker-Verlags etwa in Hugendubel- und Thalia-Filialen aus. „Wir freuen uns, dass unsere Bücher so gut ankommen", sagt Claus Arndt. Am besten verkaufen sich laut den Arndts die Lerntrainer für die Grundschule sowie für die 5. und 6. Klasse Gymnasium. Das verwundert. Claus Arndt erklärt: „Auf den jungen Schülern lastet schon eine Menge Druck."

Am besten verkaufen sich die Lerntrainer für Grundschule und 5. und 6. Klasse

Als die Arndts die Bücher in immer größerer Stückzahl verkauften, stellte sich die Frage, wie sie die Lerntrainer weiter produzieren wollen. Sie entschieden sich, die Bücher selbst zu drucken. „Alles ist handproduziert, das ist unser Markenzeichen", sagt Monika Arndt.

Sie legen Wert darauf, dass ihre Aufgaben schulnah sind und so auch wirklich abgefragt werden könnten. „Außerdem ist es wichtig für uns, die Schüler für das Lernen zu motivieren. Häufig schreiben Kinder schlechte Noten, weil sie zu wenig Selbstvertrauen haben", sagt Claus Arndt. „Wenn die Kinder mit unseren Schultrainern lernen, erkennen sie Aufgaben aus dem Unterricht wieder, das gibt ihnen ein Erfolgserlebnis und motiviert sie." Natürlich könnten die Bücher keine schon vorher entstandenen Wissenslücken schließen, „aber sie helfen, zu vertiefen und zu wiederholen."

AKTUELLES IN KÜRZE

38-Jähriger stirbt nach Drogenkonsum

Ein 38-jähriger Münchner ist am vergangenen Freitag an den Folgen von Kokain- und Alkoholkonsum gestorben. Nach Angaben der Polizei wurde der arbeitslose Münchner am Donnerstag, 17. November, in eine Klinik eingeliefert. Dort musste er reanimiert werden. In seinem Urin wurde ein hoher Kokaingehalt festgestellt. Zudem hatte er eine Alkoholvergiftung. Die Obduktion ergab, dass der 38-Jährige an einer Überdosis Rauschgift gestorben war. Die Polizei schließt Fremdverschulden aus. pm

Rechte und Pflichten von Mietern

Viele Auseinandersetzungen zwischen Vermietern und Mietern resultieren daraus, dass die Parteien ihre Rechte und Pflichten nicht kennen oder diese falsch einschätzen. Die Rechtsanwältin Gisela Weber vom Mieterverein München erläutert bei einem Infoabend im Bauzentrum München, Willy-Brandt-Allee 10, am Dienstag, 13. Dezember, ab 18 Uhr, welche Klauseln Mieter vor der Unterzeichnung eines Formularmietvertrages besonders unter die Lupe nehmen sollten. Sie spricht außerdem die Probleme des Alltags an, die im täglichen Umgang zwischen den Mietvertragsparteien und den Nachbarn auftreten können. Der Eintritt ist frei. do

Mein Sohn Leander hat sich schon letztes Jahr ausschließlich mit Ihren Heften auf seine Schulaufgaben in Mathe und Englisch vorbereitet, was uns zu einem insgesamt recht entspannten ersten Schuljahr im Gymnasium verholfen hat. Wir erleben Ihre Hefte als echte Unterstützung!

„Ein Schüler hat erzählt, dass eine Aufgabe identisch mit Ihrem Heft war. Da haben Sie eine Marktlücke entdeckt. Die Durchblicker sind sehr gefragt. Wir werden geplündert."
Ein Buchhändler

„Die Durchblicker Schulaufgaben sind inzwischen unsere Topseller!"
Eine Buchhändlerin

Top! Die Schulaufgaben von bayerischen Gymnasien sind wirklich ihr Geld wert. Das gibt den Kindern Sicherheit. Klasse!

Herzlichen Dank für die prompte Zusendung von Mathematik 11. Martin hat es gut genutzt und 14 Punkte geerntet! Vielen, vielen Dank!

VOLLTREFFER !!!
Drei Aufgaben in meiner Schulaufgabe waren genau wie die aus Ihrem Buch. Ganz toll! Danke!

Großes Lob an Ihr Engagement! Die Hinweise in den ausführlichen Lösungen sind die absoluten Insidertipps!

Wir verwenden die Schulaufgaben für bayerische Gymnasien schon seit einigen Jahren. Die Trainer sind wirklich super. Das ist der Standard, der definitiv in der Schule drankommt.

Wir haben übrigens schon Mathe und Englisch für die 5. Klasse Gymnasium zu Hause und sind total begeistert. Meine Tochter hat schon drei Einser geschrieben.

Die Tipps zu den Matheaufgaben haben meinem Sohn so viel Selbstbewusstsein gegeben, dass er in seiner Schulaufgabe die Note 1 geschrieben hat.

„Ich empfehle die Reihe immer weiter. Sie haben in mir einen Fan gefunden."
Eine Buchhändlerin

Ihre Bücher sind sensationell, wie ein treuer Wegbegleiter!

Ein dickes Lob! Meine Tochter ist absolut begeistert. Sie hat bei Physik und Chemie das Gefühl: „Das habe ich jetzt verstanden."

Guten Tag, wir haben im vergangenen Jahr mehrere Ihrer Bücher gekauft und waren sehr beeindruckt von der Qualität und dem Einklang mit dem bayrischen Gymnasium Curriculum. Nun möchten wir das für das kommende Schuljahr wiederholen.

Wir haben alle Ihre Bücher. Die sind spitze!

ISBN: 978-3-00-036559-1

9 783000 365591

Englisch 8

€ 14,95 (D) € 15,40 (A)